Dedication:

We dedicate this book to our family and hope to reignite the teachings of our ancestors so they can be carried onto future generations. And to teachers and students who are eager to know more about Indigenous culture.

We are honoured to share our interpretation of the Medicine Wheel teachings, as taught to us by Elder Francis Whiskeyjack.

Territory Acknowledgement:

The authors and Medicine Wheel Publishing respectfully acknowledge that this book was developed on the traditional territories of the Coast Salish Peoples including the Sc'ianew, Lekwungen, and T'Sou-ke Peoples; as well as on Treaty No. 6 Territory, the ancestral and traditional territory of the Cree, Dene, Blackfoot, Saulteaux, Nakota Sioux, Iroquois, Ojibway/Saulteaux/Anishinaabe, and Métis Peoples.

Funded by the Government of Canada   Financé par le gouvernement du Canada

Authors:

Carrie Armstrong:

Carrie is a proud Métis woman, teacher, and award-winning business woman who has founded and created an Indigenous-themed beauty product and tea company, Mother Earth Essentials, that has a mission to educate Canadians on the beauty of Indigenous culture and contributions made by Indigenous people. It is based on education and awareness and a high quality line of retail products produced from traditional plants and recipes.

Carrie worked in the cosmetic and spa industry for more than 15 years before returning to school to earn a Bachelor of Education from the University of Alberta. She taught at Amiskwaciy Academy, Edmonton's Indigenous high school. The school had a traditional plant garden that Carrie used to create hands-on learning opportunities for her students. Seeing the positive reaction from the students was inspiring, she realized the need to start showcasing the beauty of her culture.

Carrie was born and raised in Alberta, learning Aboriginal traditions from her grandmother. She is a dedicated mother of three incredible kids. For her, family comes first and is the central focus of her life.

Kelly Armstrong:

Kelly Armstrong is a Métis woman who grew up surrounded by a very large extended family in Hinton, Alberta. Having a mother and aunties who attended Residential School gave her much compassion for the issues and barriers that Indigenous people in Canada face on so many levels, and she is very grateful to her mother for having the courage to share her residential school experiences. Kelly has a background in Child and Youth Care and has spent most of her career working in various roles with vulnerable populations including as an Indigenous health worker, and educational assistant. Kelly lives in Hinton with her husband, where they enjoy camping, hiking and spending lots of time with their grandchildren.

River Langevin Armstrong:

River was born in St. Albert, Alberta - the home to many of her ancestors. River is currently a grade 6 student in Edmonton, Alberta. She is an animal lover and a social justice warrior in the making. She has loved nature since she was a small baby, and can identify a number of traditional plants and can name their properties. She loves video games and hanging out with her friends.

How to use this book:

The Medicine Wheel is a powerful symbol, and a tool to help children, as well as adults, find balance in physical, emotional, spiritual, and mental health. This book can be used in your classroom as a teacher resource, and by parents teaching their children at home. *The Medicine Wheel Workbook: Finding Your Healthy Balance* is designed for grades 2 to 6, and exercises can be adapted to suit each grade.

Throughout the book, you will find instructions for teachers and students. Where instructions are being given, each section will be marked with the following symbols to indicate who the instructions are directed towards.

When it pertains to teacher instructions, it has been labelled with the following marking.

When it pertains to students completing activities, it has been labelled with the following marking.

At the beginning and end of this workbook, there will be a self assessment for students. Please advise students that this assessment is meant to be used as a learning tool and serves only as a guiding point to look for potential opportunities to improve some health aspects in our lives. This is by no means a medical diagnosis, nor does it supply a significant look into our overall health.

License Permission:

Teachers and parents who have purchased this workbook have the right to make copies of the activities for use within their classrooms or homes. The license does not allow the book to be shared, copied or transmitted in any form for use outside of an individual home or classroom.

Acknowledgement:

It is important to acknowledge the diversity in Medicine Wheel Teachings that exist amongst Indigenous Peoples. Each perspective has value and we feel it is important to acknowledge the difference.

It is also important to acknowledge that this workbook is only an introduction to the many, many profound teachings that are derived from the Medicine Wheel.

Table of Contents:

Introduction — History of the Medicine Wheel

In Indigenous spirituality, the Medicine Wheel represents balance and connection. Stone Medicine Wheels are found across the plains of Alberta and the northern United States. These ancient forms of sacred architecture were built in the shape of a circle with a centre stone and lines or spokes of stones, radiating from the centre to the outer edge. Some Medicine Wheels measure up to 12 metres in diameter. Some say Medicine Wheels date back as far as six thousand years B.C.

Today, there are hand held Medicine Wheels made from metal rings and coloured beads or fabric, and small Medicine Wheels created in backyards and gardens. The Medicine Wheel symbolizes a holistic and balanced way of living and healing, and is a powerful teaching tool consisting of many layers of wisdom and knowledge. The architectural structure and placement of each stone in the Medicine Wheel teach us about the astronomical, ceremonial, and healing meanings in our lives. The wheel, or circle, is symbolic of the circle of life where there is no beginning and no end. At the centre of the Medicine Wheel is the Creator from which everything emanates. Without our Creator, nothing exists.

The Medicine Wheel is divided into four equal quadrants and is used in a clockwise direction following the path of the rising and setting of the sun. The four quadrants represent:

Four directions: east, south, west, north

Four seasons: spring, summer, fall, winter

Four colours: yellow, red, black, white

Four elements: earth, fire, water, air

Four plants: tobacco, sweetgrass, sage, cedar

Four stages of life: baby/child, teenager, adult, Elder

Four animals: eagle, buffalo, grizzly bear, wolf

Four health areas: physical, mental, emotional, spiritual

Getting Ready to Learn:

The Medicine Wheel symbolizes a holistic and balanced way of living and healing, and is a powerful teaching tool consisting of many layers of wisdom and knowledge.

Through understanding the teachings of the Medicine Wheel, there is an opportunity to achieve a greater healthy lifestyle. By using the Medicine Wheel, we can see areas in which we can work on, get help, or let go. Our culture and our spirituality lead us to believe that by reaching a place of true balance and a deep level of physical, emotional, mental, and spiritual self awareness, we will find a sense of the inner peace many of us yearn for.

Teacher Preparation for Activity:

Teachers, the following are some Instructions to give to your students.

Before we learn more about the Medicine Wheel, let's get organized and create your own Medicine Wheel Workbook notebooks. This will serve you well as a way to keep track of all your notes, activities, and documents. Make sure you make it your own!

See the following page for activity.

Welcome to Your Medicine Wheel Workbook!

My Identity

Name

Age

My cultural Background

My physical features

My strengths

What are some things that I can improve on?

What are some healthy goals in my life?

NORTH
White
Air
Spiritual
Winter
Sweetgrass
Elder
Wolf

WEST
Black
Water
Emotional
Fall
Cedar
Adult
Grizzly Bear

EAST
Yellow
Earth
Physical
Spring
Tobacco
Baby
Eagle

SOUTH
Red
Fire
Mental
Summer
Sage
Teenager
Buffalo

How to Introduce The Medicine Wheel

When introducing the Medicine Wheel to your students or children, start with explaining the teaching board concepts first and what they represent.

For example,

Colour: Red
Direction: South
Element: Fire
Health: Mental
Season: Summer
Plant: Sage
Stage of Life: Teenager
Animal: Buffalo

Teacher Led Discussion:

Start with a discussion in general about circles and cycles, having students brainstorm all the circles/cycles they can think of, activating prior knowledge to help in understanding concepts.

Possible ideas:

Circles in nature — Planets orbit the Sun, the Moon orbits the Earth, the Earth spins in a circle and is round, we see the Sun and Moon move in a circle around the Earth, seasons cycle, water cycles, plant and animal life cycles, death leads to new life. For example, a fruit falls from the tree, rots and dies, and then the seeds grow into a new tree.

Our life cycle starts as a newborn needing to be taken care of, ends as an elder that may need physical assistance with many things; we may feel that we've solved a problem for ourselves only for the problem to pop up again — like relationships with friends going through cycles of closeness and frustration and then making up again.

Our society has a rhythm and cycle (starting school, Christmas break, spring break, summer vacation, and repeat; our parents have children, the children grow up to have their own kids and the parents become grandparents, and the children become parents…).

Circles are sacred because they are so significant in our lives and if you look carefully you can see them everywhere. There are many things we can learn from the circles and processes.

Write out the different examples of circles and cycles on the board to prep for the next activity.

Note: As the Medicine Wheel is a sacred symbol, it is important the discussion remains respectful.

Activity 1 - Circles

Inside the circles below, draw four different pictures, or cycles
that take place in nature.

For older grades, write how that circle or cycle impacts you.

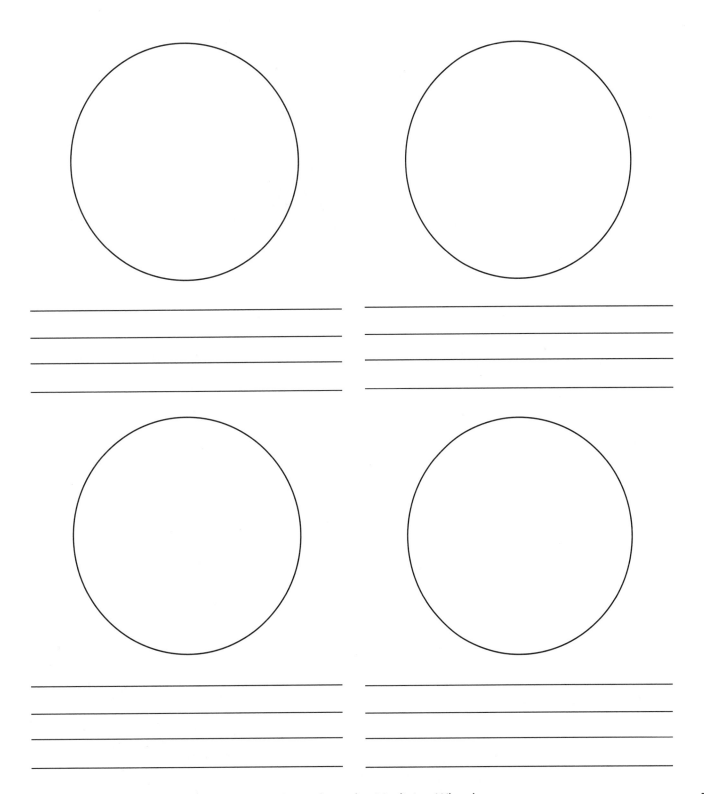

Discussion:

The Medicine Wheel is built in a circle, and there are some cycles within that circle as well.

The wheel (circle) is divided into four equal sections or quadrants. Many people relate to those as the four directions. Four is a very significant number in our culture and the Medicine Wheel teachings contain the sacred teachings of four.

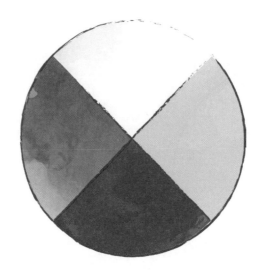

We have four directions (east, south, west, north); four seasons (spring, summer, autumn, winter); four races of people (yellow, red, black, white); four elements, (fire, earth, water, air); four sacred plants (tobacco, sage, cedar, sweetgrass); four stages of life (baby, teen, adult, elder).

Please note: Students do not need to understand all of the information in each quadrant in depth. It will continue to be explored throughout the book.

Direction	East	North	West	South
Colour	Yellow	White	Black	Red
Element	Earth	Air	Water	Fire
Health	Physical	Spiritual	Emotional	Mental
Season	Spring	Winter	Fall	Summer
Sacred Plant	Tobacco	Sweetgrass	Cedar	Sage
Stage of Life	Baby	Elder	Adult	Teenager
Animal	Eagle	Wolf	Grizzly Bear	Buffalo

Matching Activity

Draw a circle around one of the directions then make a line to the corresponding animal, colour, season, and health-related area. If needed, please refer to the guide found at the beginning of the chapter. An example is shown for you below.

Direction	Animal	Colour	Season	Health Area
East	Buffalo	Black	Fall	(Spiritual)
South	Grizzly Bear	Yellow	Spring	Mental
(North)	Eagle	Red	(Winter)	Physical
West	(Wolf)	(White)	Summer	Emotional

Activity 2 - Medicine Wheel Fill in the Blanks

With the help of the teachings board, fill in the Medicine Wheel with each of the proper concepts. Shade in each section with the matching colour.

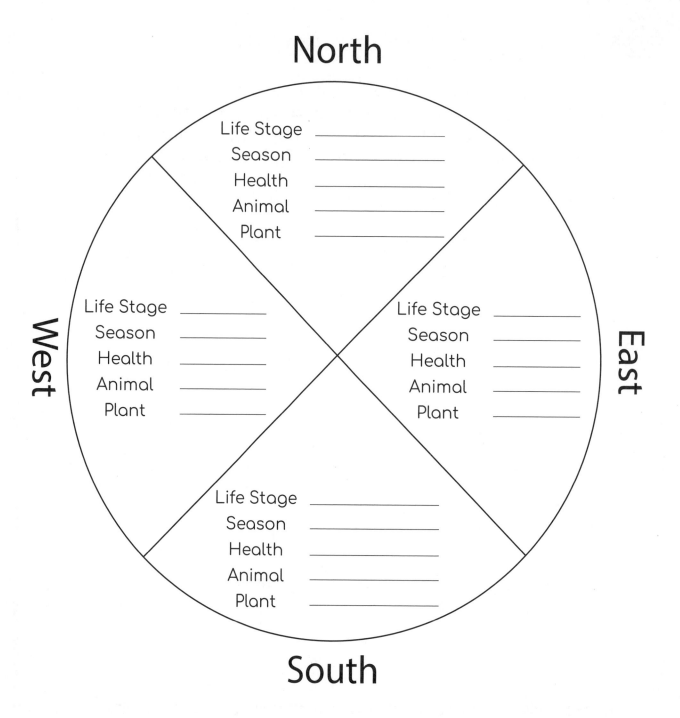

North

West

East

South

Life Stage _____
Season _____
Health _____
Animal _____
Plant _____

Life Stage _____
Season _____
Health _____
Animal _____
Plant _____

Life Stage _____
Season _____
Health _____
Animal _____
Plant _____

Life Stage _____
Season _____
Health _____
Animal _____
Plant _____

The Medicine Wheel and a Healthy Balance:

The Medicine Wheel has many, many teachings. One teaching is to learn to live in a balanced, healthy way. Each of the four colours of the Medicine Wheel represents the physical, emotional, mental, and spiritual areas of our life. The following self assessment is designed to see where students are starting at physically, emotionally, mentally, and spiritually.

Please let students know that the answers are a rough idea for establishing health. They are designed to help us see where we could improve, and are not meant to judge on whether they are a good person or not. Learning to teach our children about self reflection and assessing oneself, while not being judgemental or unkind to oneself, is important in maintaining a healthy balance.

At the end of the book, students will repeat the self assessment to see how exploring the teachings of the Medicine Wheel may have impacted their overall outlook of health.

Do I live in a healthy balance?

Check YES or NO to the following questions.

Remember, this is only one way to determine health, and the answers are there to help us do better when we may need to.

Physical

I exercise 2-3 times a week on a regular basis   YES ☐ NO ☐

I eat a balanced, nutritious diet on a regular basis   YES ☐ NO ☐

I drink 6-8 cups of water a day   YES ☐ NO ☐

I sleep well every night   YES ☐ NO ☐

Total number of YES responses in this section   ☐

Emotional

I have supportive family and/or friends in my life   YES ☐ NO ☐

I share my feelings openly and appropriately   YES ☐ NO ☐

I have healthy ways to deal with stress   YES ☐ NO ☐

I am comfortable asking for help when I need it   YES ☐ NO ☐

Total number of YES responses in this section   ☐

Mental

I enjoy learning new things   YES ☐ NO ☐

I can analyze what I read or watch   YES ☐ NO ☐

I contribute to my community   YES ☐ NO ☐

I challenge myself   YES ☐ NO ☐

Total number of YES responses in this section   [   ]

Spiritual

I have an insightful and nurturing relationship with myself
and others   YES ☐ NO ☐

I have a strong personal value system   YES ☐ NO ☐

I feel like I have a purpose in life   YES ☐ NO ☐

I set aside time for solitude and deep thought   YES ☐ NO ☐

Total number of YES responses in this section   [   ]

Scores:

Reflect on your total number of YES responses for each section.

If you scored 0 or 1 out of 4, maybe there are some things you can do to improve your health in that area. Choose one or two NOs and turn those into a YES!

If you scored 2 out of 4, you are doing some things in a healthy way. Great start! Do you think it is possible to change one NO and turn it into a YES?

If you scored 3 out of 4 then you are surely living in a healthy way.

If you scored 4 out of 4. Wow! You are already doing so much.

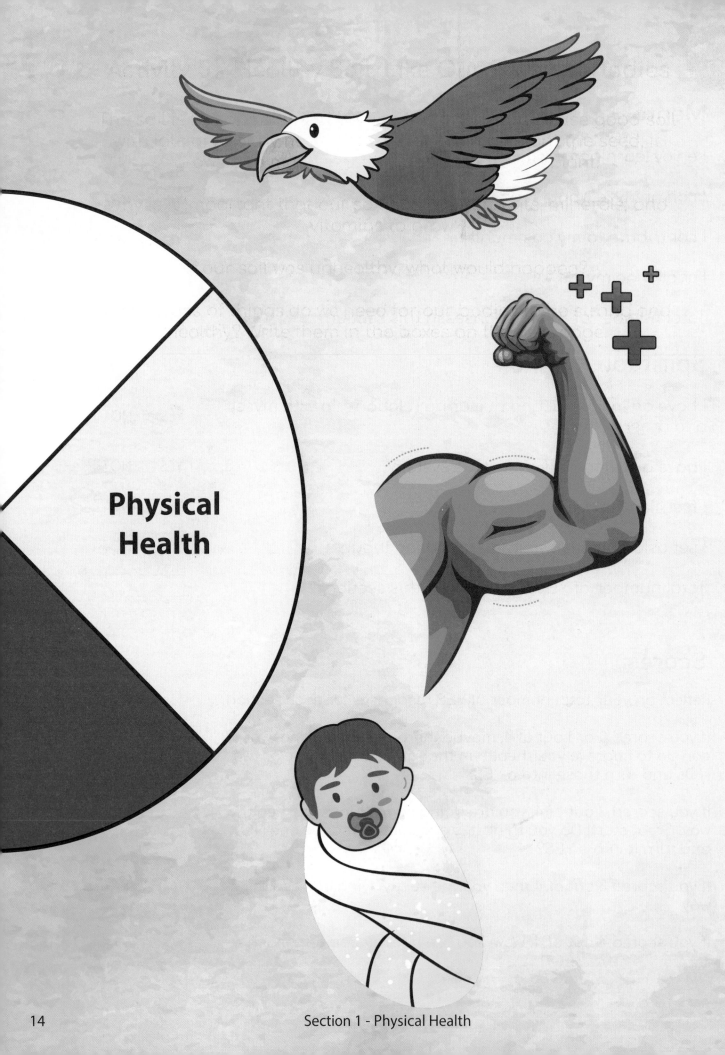

Physical Health

Section 1 - Physical Health

Rising in the east, the blazing yellow sun represents a new day, new life, birth, beginnings, and our physical birth. We were babies then. We can also think of birth as a season, which is spring. When you think of spring, you think of growth and new beginnings, new life. Our physical selves begin when we are born.

Direction	**East**
Colour	Yellow
Element	Earth
Health	Physical
Season	Spring
Sacred Plant	Tobacco
Stage of Life	Baby
Animal	Eagle

Activity 1 - Reflection

Complete each sentence in your own words:

When the sun rises, I am greeted with _____ .

The blazing yellow sun of a new day
introduces me to _____ .

When I think of Spring, I feel _____ .

Rising in the east, the blazing yellow sun represents a new day, new life, birth, beginnings, and our physical birth. We were babies then. We can also think of birth as a season, which is spring. When you think of spring you think of growth and new beginnings, new life. Our physical selves begin in the east.

In the box below, draw a picture of what an eagle will see when it is flying above during springtime. You can choose to include plants, birds, trees, etc...

Activity 2 - Plant Cycles

As Eagle watches from above, springtime begins. The eagle oversees the renewal of new life — it is his responsibility. Eagle is Mother Earth's messenger. Springtime leads to the renewal of flowers and trees, rivers, etc... One of the big physical changes can be found in the process of a seed becoming a tree or a plant.

In the circle below, draw your favourite plant, tree or flower that you get to see during springtime.

Activity 2 - Continued

The plant life cycle is the same as our physical life cycle.
Illustrate this in the box. Show the similarities.

Plant Cycle	Human Cycle

Activity 3 - Respecting Mother Earth

Mother Earth provides us with nourishment for our physical growth. We eat plants and animals from birth to death, but we also use them as medicine. Our Elders have taught us which plants are good in times of need. Tobacco is one of those sacred plants that we can use to give back to Mother Earth when something is taken.

What are some of the gifts that Mother Earth provides us with? Draw and label these gifts in the circle below.

Activity 4 - Physical Activities for Growth

Take time to reflect on your physical growth from birth to 12 years of age.

Now also think about what types of physical activities would a baby, teenager, adult or elder do during their respective ages?

Life Stage	Types Of Activities
Baby	
Teenager	
Adult	
Elder	

If the baby never did any physical activity or movement, what would happen to the baby? _____

What about a teenager? _____

What about the adult? _____

What about an elder? _____

Choose one activity that you would really love to do and be able to do at your age.

What is the activity? _____

Activity 5 - Healthy Soil, Like Our Physical Bodies

The soil is like our physical bodies. It is important to use good soil with lots of healthy nutrients so that when we plant the seed, it grows and matures into a beautiful tree or plant.

Why is it important that our soil has the nutrients, minerals, and vitamins to grow?

If our soil was unhealthy, what would happen?

What types of things do we need for our bodies to be strong and healthy? Write them in the boxes on the next page.

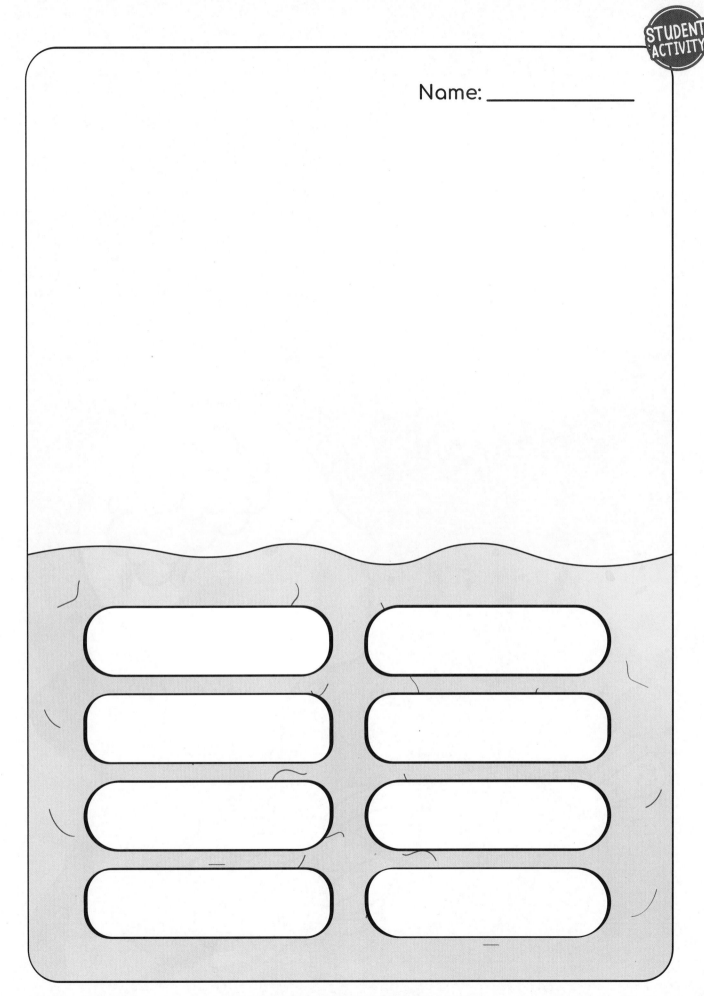

Name: _____

Mental

Section 2 - Mental Health

The south quadrant of the Medicine Wheel represents the summer and the warmth of full day sun. At this point, the seeds have grown from babies/kids to teenagers. It is a time for growth and development — adolescence. This quadrant represents the mental aspect. When we get to the teenage years, we start to use our mind a lot more.

Direction	South
Colour	Red
Element	Fire
Type of Education	Mental
Season	Summer
Sacred Plant	Sage
Stage of Life	Teenager
Animal	Buffalo

Activity 1 - Reflection

The warmth of summer reminds me of _____.

The stages of birth and childhood I am in, or I have just completed. Next, the teenage years are ahead and I feel _____ because _____.

There will be several mental obstacles that I will encounter as I move into adolescence/teenage years. I feel the challenges may be _____ and _____ because_____.

List some ways that you feel you can be mindful, to help you prepare for these mental challenges that may come in the teenage years.

_____

_____

_____

_____

_____

_____

_____

_____

_____

_____

Activity 2 - Fire

Fire represents the mental and emotional challenges for teenagers.

Do you feel the teachings from your parents and grandparents are preparing you for this stage of life?

Fires are powerful and dangerous when out of control. Learning to control fire is important and requires balance.

A forest fire rapidly spreads across lands and burns uncontrollably for extended periods of time. This can be compared to the challenges this stage brings. Activities to control your forest fire are the things you do to regulate and maintain a calm mind.

What kinds of activities can you do to control your forest fire? List four in the boxes.

Examples: reading, exercising, sports, music.

One activity that is hard to do is _____ because_____.

Draw yourself trying one of the activities.

Activity 3 - Buffalo Strong

While I am growing up, I will face many challenges and my mind can overcome them. I know my mind can be strong like the Buffalo.

The activity that keeps me mentally strong and shows my strength is
_____.

I need to think positive while I do this activity because _____.

Write positive words into the image of the buffalo below.

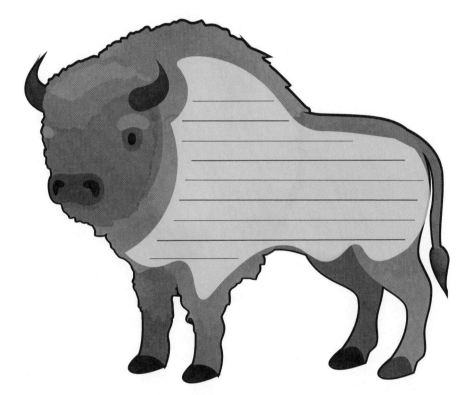

I can overcome my fires/challenges using the power of my mind and believing in myself.

Think of an activity that you find particularly challenging and list it below.

_____

Using your mind and your thoughts, you can achieve goals even if they are challenging. What are things you can say to yourself to help you achieve your goal?

1. _____

2. _____

3. _____

Activity 4 - Healthy and Happy Minds

A plant needs many things to grow healthy and happy. The soil represents our physical selves, and we know what it takes to keep our bodies healthy. Every plant needs the warmth of the sun to grow. The sun can be associated with heat or fire. The warmth of the sun helps the plant to grow, just like our minds grow. Our mind's activities, or fire, can be gentle and help the plant to grow, but if the fire is too much, it can harm or burn the plant.

What type of things do we need for our mind to be healthy? Write them in the boxes coming out from the sun.

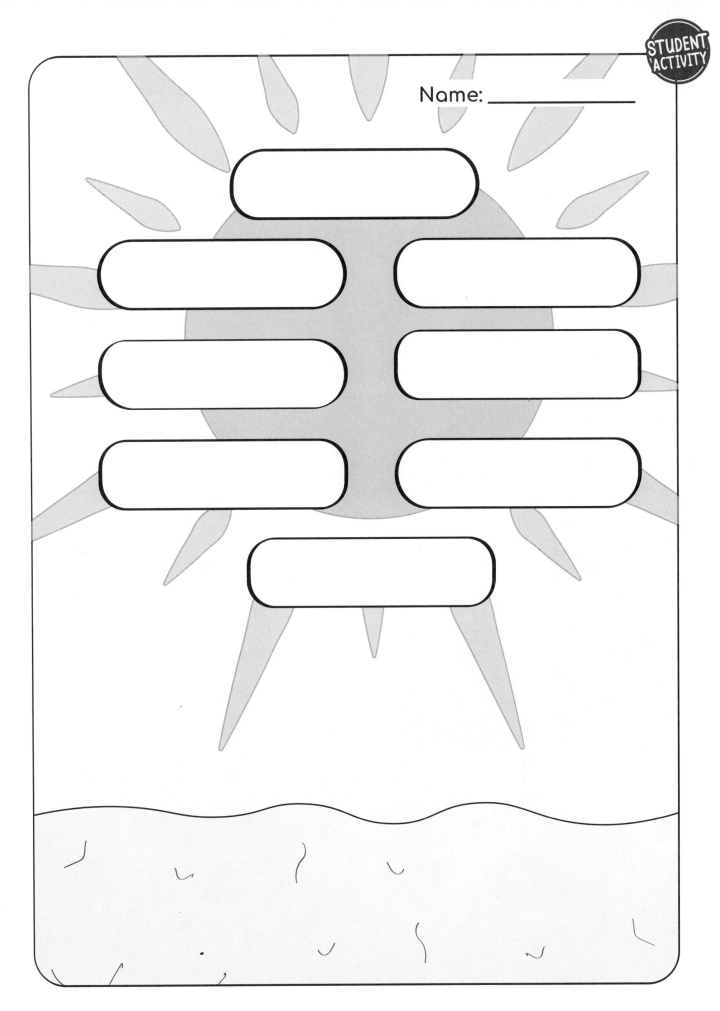

Section 3 - Emotional Health

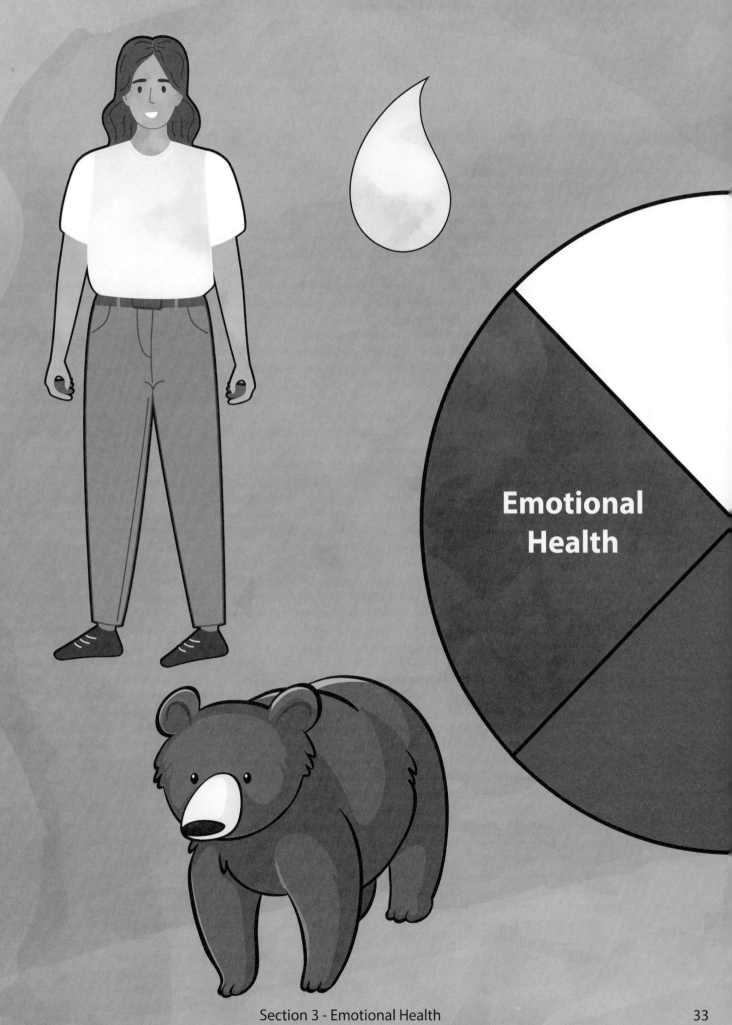

Section 3 - Emotional Health

The next stage of the Medicine Wheel after south is the west. It represents the autumn season and the black of night. The teenagers then become adults; this is the emotional part of life. It is a time for harvest and deeper understanding — adulthood.

Direction	**West**
Colour	Black
Element	Water
Health	Emotional
Season	Fall
Sacred Plant	Cedar
Stage of Life	Adult
Animal	Grizzly Bear

Activity 1 - Colour Reflection

As fall begins, Mother Earth shows many beautiful colours. She splashes rich colours of gold, orange, purple, and shades of brown too.

Gold - Energy   Purple - Love

Brown - Relaxed   Orange - Joy

How do these colours show your feelings?

Place your pencil in the middle of each circle and move it around (staying within the lines) as if you were drawing the feeling listed.

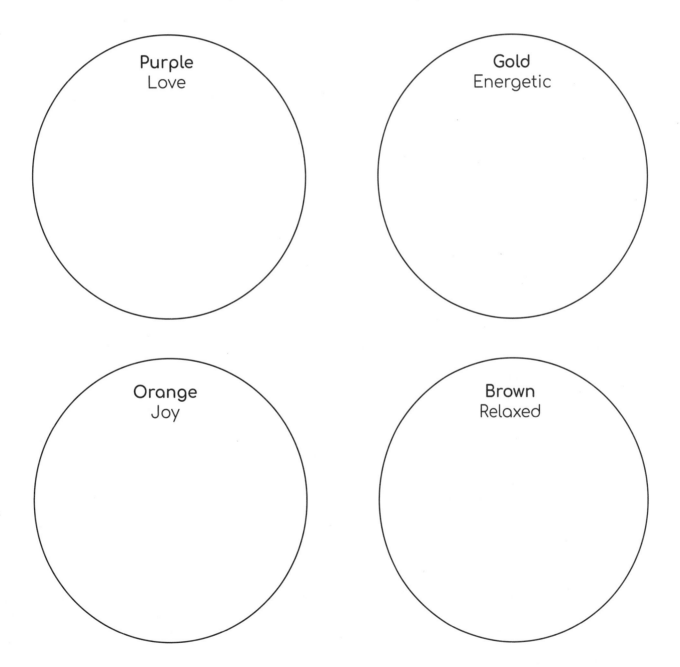

Purple
Love

Gold
Energetic

Orange
Joy

Brown
Relaxed

Activity 2 - Water

Feelings and emotions help us to share how we feel in different situations. As water runs down a river, the ripples are always changing — just like our feelings.

Anger

Bored

Relaxed

Calm

Draw your face showing these feelings

Anger

Bored

Relaxed

Calm

Activity 3 - Gifts of Cedar

Mother Earth gives us the sacred plant of cedar to help process our emotions. When we use cedar as smudge, we are asking for our hearts to be cleansed and to restore balance to our feelings. The cedar tree carries powerful medicine to help us balance our feelings.

Draw a cedar tree below using the picture as your guide. Colour it when you're done.

Activity 4 - Likes/Dislikes

Food fuels our body. We need to eat a mixture of fruits, vegetables, whole grains, and protein to keep our body strong and healthy. Unhealthy foods should be enjoyed once in a while, while healthy foods are to be enjoyed every day. Have students work with partners for 5 minutes to brainstorm a list of healthy and unhealthy foods. Then have each set of partners share one of each. Teacher records on the Smartboard or whiteboard. Then have students complete the list of healthy and unhealthy foods.

Make a list of healthy and unhealthy foods.

Put a ✔ by the foods you like and ✘ by the foods you don't like

Healthy   Unhealthy

Do you notice a difference in how you feel when you eat healthy food versus non healthy foods?
Remember our feelings are connected to our physical bodies.

Other activity ideas:
Using grocery store flyers, have students create a collage of pictures of healthy and unhealthy foods.
OR
Have students create a PowerPoint or Word document with pictures of healthy and unhealthy foods.

Activity 5 - Grizzly Bear

There are many bears in our world: polar bears, brown bears, black bears, etc... Yet, there is one bear, the Grizzly bear, that is connected to the teaching of solitude and meditation. The grizzly bear's territory is vast and they need a lot of space to live a full life. The space the grizzly bear lives in is quiet and peaceful, and he likes his space from other bears. This allows the grizzly bear the space to feel calm and at ease.

a.) How is Grizzly Bear feeling during his alone time?

_____
_____
_____
_____

b.) When you are alone, how do you feel?

_____
_____
_____
_____

c.) Just like the grizzly bear, do you think it is wise to take time for yourself? What are the benefits of choosing to listen to your feelings when you are alone?

_____
_____
_____
_____

d.) Some people like being alone to read a book, colour or think. Some people like to be around lots of other people to feel good inside. Do you know which one you are?

_____
_____
_____
_____

Activity 6 - Still Growing

We began as soil (earth), then we learned about the importance of the sun (fire), and now it is time for water. The plant cannot survive without water. If a plant does not receive water it would slowly die. Water, like our feelings, is very important to our growth as human beings.

What types of things do we need for our hearts and feelings to be healthy?

Write them in the boxes on the following page.

Section 3 - Emotional Health

STUDENT ACTIVITY

Spiritual

Section 4 - Spiritual Health

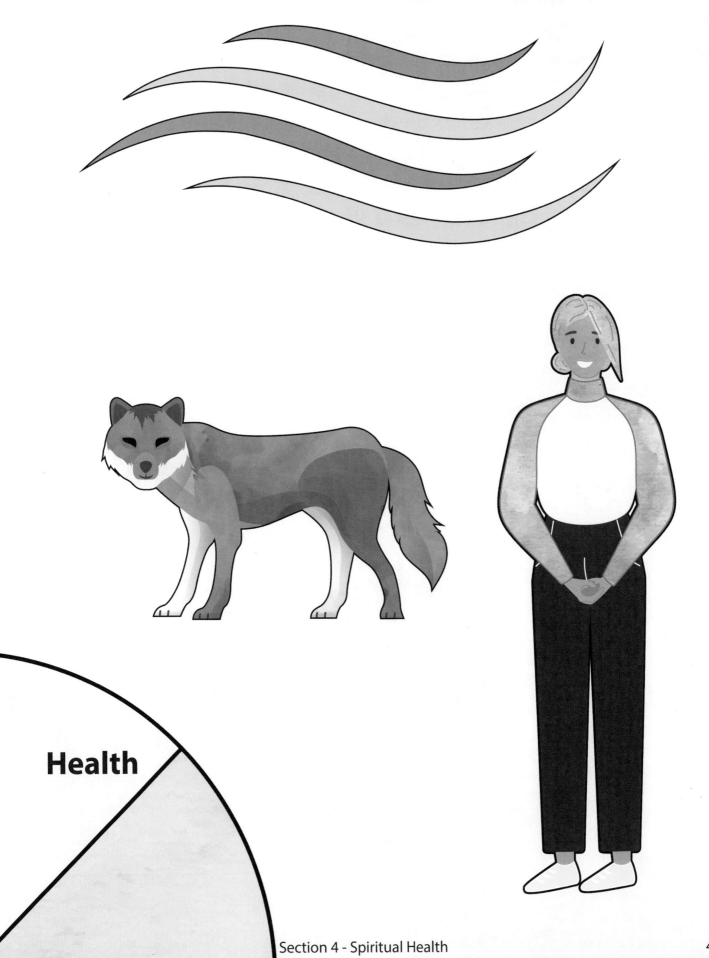

Health

Section 4 - Spiritual Health

The north is seen as the season of winter, snow, and cold. It represents the Elder's white hair. To many Elders, spirituality is very important. The seeds are carried on throughout the lifecycle. This is a place for reflecting and understanding life — old age.

Direction	**North**
Colour	White
Element	Air
Health	Spiritual
Season	Winter
Sacred Plant	Sweetgrass
Stage of Life	Elder
Animal	Wolf

Activity 1 - Elder's Wisdom

Indigenous communities have Elders (men/women) who share teachings, ceremonies, and stories of long ago.

In non-Indigenous communities and families, this role is usually filled by a grandparent or other trusted and respected adult who may hold the qualities of an Elder.

Complete these sentences:

1. An Elder is _____.

2. An Elder shares his/her stories about _____.

3. They have taught me about _____ and _____.

4. An Elder is important in my community_____.

Choose 1 activity to complete:

   a.) Interview an Elder - prepare your questions and seek advice from your parent/s about protocol.

   b.) Write a brief description of an Elder from your community. For the purpose of these activities, if you do not have an Elder to connect with, any trusted and respected adult who may hold the qualities of an Elder is okay.

Activity 2 - Winter Stories

Long ago, stories or legends were shared by Elders and grandparents during the winter season.

On a separate piece of paper, write a short story about a favourite time with your grandparent/s.
Younger students may draw a picture and label it.

a.) Where did the story take place?

_____

_____

b.) Who was there?

_____

_____

c.) What were you doing?

_____

_____

d.) How did you feel?

_____

_____

e.) Why do you remember this story?

_____

_____

Draw the setting of your story.

Activity 3 - I Am the Wolf

The wolf knows their purpose in their pack community. He/she values their role and carries themselves in a good way. To harm the pack is one of the worst things a wolf can do. Just like a family or pack, every wolf plays a different role.

In the circle below, read the description of each role and check mark the ones that speak to the role you play in your pack. If you do not know what these terms mean, ask an Elder or trusted adult.

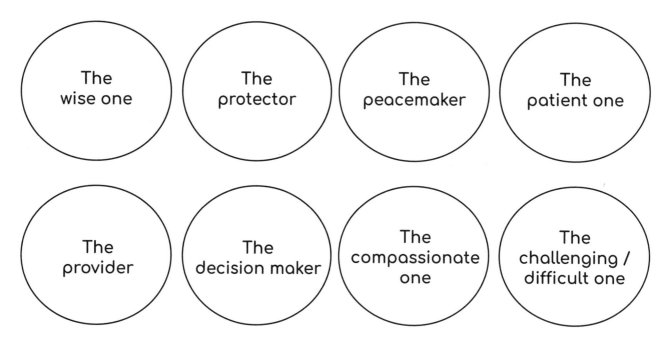

The wise one

The protector

The peacemaker

The patient one

The provider

The decision maker

The compassionate one

The challenging / difficult one

Are there any other roles you feel that you play within your pack? Write them in the circles below.

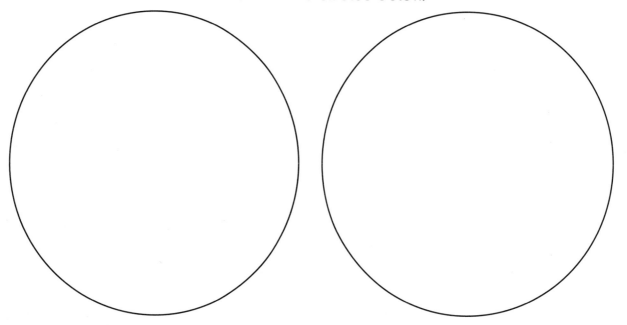

Activity 4 - My Values

Values are the things that are most important to you and what you care about. These values guide your choices and help you to live a happy and balanced life.

List four values and draw each one into the boxes below.
To help you get started, we've provided a list of values to choose from, or you may include any of your own values that are important to you.

Kindness, Caring, Being Strong, Honesty, Truthfulness, Patience, Love, Assertiveness, Helpfulness, Independence, Loyalty, Peacefulness, Service, Friendship, Balance, Courage, Hope, Harmony, Grace, Tradition, Vision, Wisdom, Humility, Respect, Open mindedness, Empathy, Confidence, Gratitude, etc...

1. _____

2. _____

3. _____

4. _____

Your Values Worksheet:

Complete the following worksheet and write your own values in the blank spaces.

	Important	Sort of Important	Not Important
Community	☐	☐	☐
Family	☐	☐	☐
Kindness	☐	☐	☐
Fun	☐	☐	☐
Health	☐	☐	☐
Helping Others	☐	☐	☐
Creativity	☐	☐	☐
Respect	☐	☐	☐
_____	☐	☐	☐
_____	☐	☐	☐
_____	☐	☐	☐
_____	☐	☐	☐

Activity 5 - Wisdom

We know that every plant needs earth (soil), fire (warmth from the sun) and water to grow healthy and strong. There is one more element that helps plants to grow and that is air. Air has oxygen and plants need air to grow and develop. Air, like our spirituality and our values, helps us to grow.

What kinds of things do we need to live a healthy and value based life?

Write them in the boxes coming from the air in the following activity.

Activity 6 - Healthy Spirit, Healthy Me

We now know that keeping our spirit healthy is an important piece of our overall health. A healthy spirit can look and feel different to different people, and we can work to achieve a healthy spirit in many different ways.

The following are suggestions of some ways we can keep our spirit healthy. Choosing 1 or 2 of the suggestions, write about how or why these speak to you. How do they make you feel? How could they help you in your journey to spiritual health?

1. Listen to an Elder's Story
2. Sing, listen to, or play your favourite music
3. Volunteer or help others
4. Spend time in nature
5. Yoga/meditation/deep breathing
6. Participate in faith-based activities or services
7. Keep a journal/self-reflection
8. Be grateful/count your blessings
9. Do a good deed/random act of kindness
10. Step away from electronics/social media

1st Activity: _____

_____

_____

_____

2nd Activity: _____

_____

_____

_____

Are there any other things not suggested that you feel would help to keep your spirit healthy?

_____

_____

_____

Finding **Your**

Section 5 - Finding Your Healthy Balance

Healthy

Balance

Section 5 - Finding Your Healthy Balance

You have started studying physical, mental, emotional and spiritual health teachings from the Medicine Wheel. Now it's time to start connecting all the pieces, and see how these teachings come together and impact our overall health.

Let's see what you remember so far. Using the words provided, write each one into the section of the Medicine Wheel where it belongs. Refer to the teachings board concept page if needed.

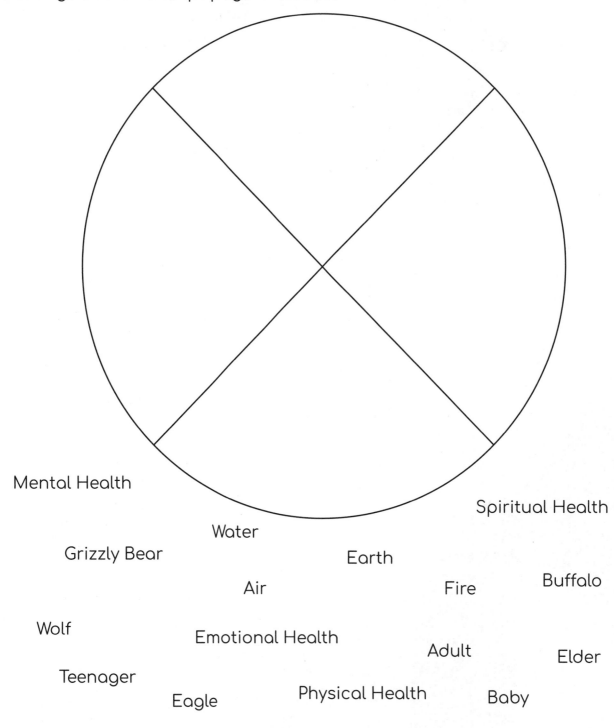

Mental Health

Spiritual Health

Water

Grizzly Bear

Earth

Buffalo

Air

Fire

Wolf

Emotional Health

Adult

Elder

Teenager

Eagle

Physical Health

Baby

Activity 1 - Physical Health

We have learned about the four quadrants of the Medicine Wheel. Now, it's time to explore the effects that being physically active has on our emotional, mental, and spiritual selves. Choose one physical activity. After completing the activity write down the mental, emotional, physical, and spiritual benefits of how you feel in each area.

My Physical Activity : _____

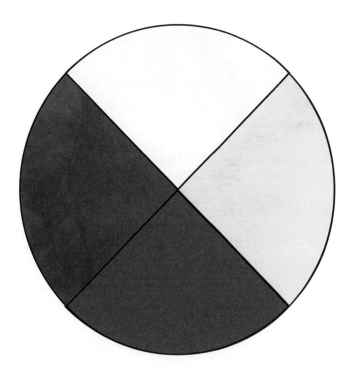

After the physical activity, write down how you are feeling physically, emotionally, mentally, and spiritually.

Physical	Mental	Emotional	Spiritual

Activity 2 - Mindfulness Activity

Mindfulness is being aware of how we are feeling in our bodies, minds, and hearts. Mindfulness helps us balance ourselves physically, mentally, emotionally, and spiritually.

Create a relaxing atmosphere inside or outside the classroom.

Begin by:

1.) Play flute/music in background or in nature
2.) Use one of these ideas as guided imagery

Colour Breathing - ask students to think of a relaxing colour and another colour that represents anger, frustration or sadness. Close eyes and imagine they are breathing in the relaxing colour and filling their entire bodies. On the exhale, ask them to picture the "negative" colour leaving their body and releasing it through the area or room.

3.) Have students do a body scan. What are you feeling in your body, heart, and mind?

Teacher Ideas to increase mindfulness and encourage the development of healthy minds in our students and children:

1.) Daily Gratitude - Before the students are dismissed at the end of the day, they can be given an "exit slip" where they write down what they are thankful for during a physical activity they participated in and hand it back to the teacher.

2.) Gratitude Corner - Have small cards (3" x 4") available for students to express gratitude to a classmate. Students write their thank you on the card, and give it to that classmate. They can then be posted on a bulletin board.

3.) Gratitude Journal - Have students write something they are grateful for at the end of every day.

It is important to remind students that there is no "right" way to express gratitude.

Activity 3 - Showing Gratitude

Complete the following sentences.

Inside of myself, I am grateful for...

_____

_____

I am proud that...

_____

_____

Outside of myself, I am grateful for...

_____

_____

When I feel grateful my body feels...

_____

_____

When I feel grateful my mind feels...

_____

_____

When I feel grateful my spirit feels...

_____

_____

Activity 4 - Emotional Sharing

Your Feelings are Important

Feelings, like water, come into your heart. Some feelings will be full of joy, while others may not. Remember to breathe and allow these feelings to pass. No feeling is a bad feeling. You are allowed to feel exactly how you feel. Every feeling is there to teach you something.

In the last week, remember two times where you felt big feelings. Draw a picture of what was happening in the circles below.

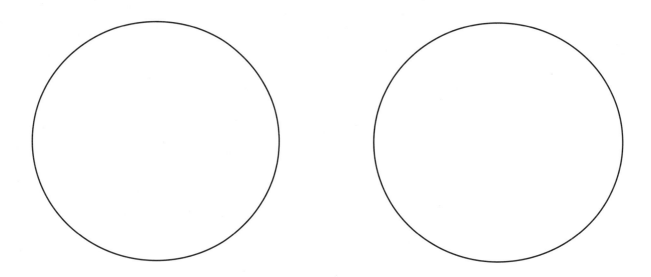

In the lines below, write about how you felt physically, emotionally and spiritually when you were feeling these big feelings.

_____   _____

_____   _____

_____   _____

_____   _____

Activity 5 - Sharing Your Feelings in the Sharing Circle

We are all part of a community. To learn to be together as part of a community may require some practise in communication. And learning to communicate your feelings is very important. A great way to practise this is in the Sharing Circle. The Sharing Circle brings all people together in one circle to share.

Step 1 - Have everyone join a circle. The circle is very important as it shows that everyone is equal and connected to each other.

Step 2 - Choose something to be passed around as the talking stick. Unless you have the talking stick, you should not be speaking.

Step 3 - It is important that everyone listen. When the talking stick comes to you, you can choose to speak or pass the talking stick.

Step 4 - When sharing, practise sharing your feelings, if you feel safe to do so. You can say things like "I feel _____ because _____." Try to avoid statements about other people and focus on your feelings.

Step 5 - After the sharing circle make sure you thank everyone for sharing and being together.

Take notice of how you feel physically, mentally, emotionally, and spiritually when you share what you are thinking and feeling, as well as when you listen, in the sharing circle.

Spiritual Health Activity - Mindfulness or Meditation

Daily meditations for mindfulness can be based on gifts from Mother Earth — seasons (winter, spring, summer, fall), animals (eagle, grizzly bear, wolf, buffalo), elements (air, earth, fire, water), and colours (white, yellow, red, black).

These meditations can be used to begin or close the day.

These starters can be used

Good morning/ evening Grandmothers and Grandfathers.
Today, I am thankful for _____

There are many guided meditations available. Please feel free to use the following:

Rest your body on the ground or find a comfortable place to sit. Let's start with your physical body. Notice what your body is touching. Notice the ground beneath you. Allow your body to slowly become a part of the ground beneath you. To be a part of Mother Earth. Take a deep breath in and allow your body and the ground to be one. As you go deeper and deeper into Mother Earth, imagine a beautiful tree or plant.

That tree or plant did not start there. It started as a tiny, tiny, tiny seed. To grow, it needs many things. To grow you need that soil. You need beautiful, rich, and healthy soil to grow. Plant that seed into that beautiful soil. Continue to take deep breaths, breathing in and out.

You have the physical needs of that seed met. You are the seed planted in beautiful soil. Now, feel that warmth of the sun's ray shining on you. You can feel the warmth, the fire from the sun. Like the power of your mind, the heat from the sun continues to warm the seed. Deep breaths in and out.

You have soil. You have warmth. Now you need water for your seed to grow. Imagine a stream flowing close to where you planted your seed. Like the stream, your feelings also flow like water… allow your feelings to flow. Breathe in and out. Deep Breaths. Imagine some of that water flowing over the seed.

Soil. Sunlight. Water. Now the seed needs air. Oxygen is needed to grow to be healthy and strong. The air flows in and around the soil, giving the seed what it needs. The air is like meditation, quietness, and calmness. Deep breath in.

Imagine with Earth (from the soil), Fire (from the sun), Water, and Air — the seed can grow. Imagine the seed taking in all of these beautiful elements and turning into a healthy beautiful tree or plant.

You are just like the seed. To be healthy and strong you need to take care of your physical, mental, emotional, and spiritual self. Grow strong. Grow Healthy. Become the mighty tree or beautiful plant that you are meant to be.

Activity 6 - Retake the Assessment

Now that you have learned about the health of your physical, mental, emotional, and spiritual selves, it's time to take the self assessment on the following page. Remember, learning how to be healthy is a constant ongoing process.

Be kind to yourself.

Be healthy.

"You are just like the seed. To be healthy and strong you need to take care of your physical, mental, emotional and spiritual self. Grow strong. Grow healthy. Become the mighty tree or beautiful plant that you are meant to be."

Do I live in a healthy balance?

Check YES or NO to the following questions.

Remember, this is only one way to determine health, and the answers are there to help us do better when we may need to.

Physical

I exercise 2-3 times a week on a regular basis	YES ☐	NO ☐
I eat a balanced, nutritious diet on a regular basis	YES ☐	NO ☐
I drink 6-8 cups of water a day	YES ☐	NO ☐
I sleep well every night	YES ☐	NO ☐
Total number of YES responses in this section		☐

Emotional

I have supportive family and/or friends in my life	YES ☐	NO ☐
I share my feelings openly and appropriately	YES ☐	NO ☐
I have healthy ways to deal with stress	YES ☐	NO ☐
I am comfortable asking for help when I need it	YES ☐	NO ☐
Total number of YES responses in this section		☐

Mental

I enjoy learning new things   YES ☐ NO ☐

I can analyze what I read or watch   YES ☐ NO ☐

I contribute to my community   YES ☐ NO ☐

I challenge myself   YES ☐ NO ☐

Total number of YES responses in this section   ☐

Spiritual

I have an insightful and nurturing relationship with myself
and others   YES ☐ NO ☐

I have a strong personal value system   YES ☐ NO ☐

I feel like I have a purpose in life   YES ☐ NO ☐

I set aside time for solitude and deep thought   YES ☐ NO ☐

Total number of YES responses in this section   ☐

Scores:

Reflect on your total number of YES responses for each section.

If you scored 0 or 1 out of 4, maybe there are some things you can do to improve your health in that area. Choose one or two NOs and turn those into a YES!

If you scored 2 out of 4, you are doing some things in a healthy way. Great start! Do you think it is possible to change one NO and turn it into a YES?

If you scored 3 out of 4 then you are surely living in a healthy way.

If you scored 4 out of 4. Wow! You are already doing so much.

The Medicine Wheel has many powerful teachings that can help you on your journey in becoming healthy.

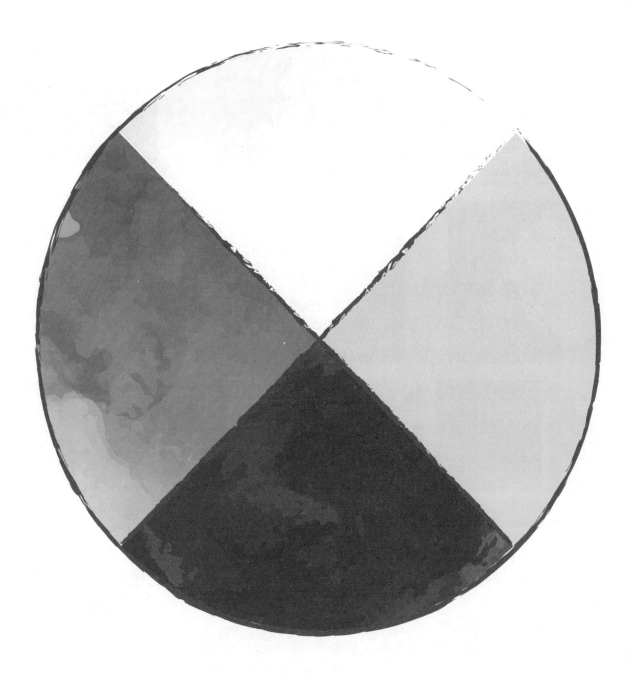

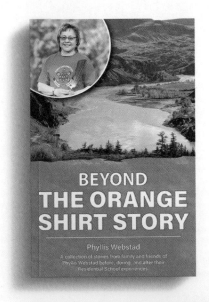

BEYOND
**THE ORANGE
SHIRT STORY**

Phyllis Webstad

A collection of stories from family and friends of Phyllis Webstad before, during, and after their Residential School experiences.

DRUM FROM THE HEART

Author: Ren Louie
Illustrator: Karlene Harvey

ORANGE SHIRT DAY
SEPTEMBER 30TH

Orange Shirt Society

Edited and Approved by
Phyllis Webstad & Joan Sorley

THIS IS WHAT
I'VE BEEN TOLD
MII YI GAA-RE-WIINDMAAGOOYAAN

We Learn
from the
Sun

David Bouchard
Paintings by Kristy Cameron

Meet Your
Family
Gikenim Giniigi'igoog

Trudy's Healing
Stone

The Hoop Dancer's
Teachings

The Eagle Feather

The Circle of Caring and Sharing

Phyllis's Orange
Shirt

Gifts from
Raven

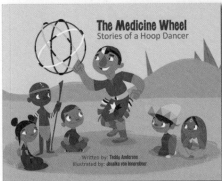

The Medicine Wheel
Stories of a Hoop Dancer

Written by: Teddy Anderson
Illustrated by: Jessika von Innerebner

RAVEN'S
FEAST

BY Kung Jaadee   ILLUSTRATED BY Jessika von Innerebner

DAWN
FLIGHT
A LAKOTA STORY

WRITTEN BY KEVIN LOCKE   ILLUSTRATED BY Jessika von Innerebner

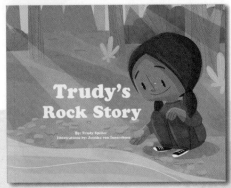

Trudy's
Rock Story

By: Trudy Spiller
Illustrations by: Jessika von Innerebner

The
SHARING
CIRCLE

Written by
Theresa "Corky" Larsen-Jonasson   Illustrated by Jessika von Innerebner

the Orange Shirt Story

Author: Phyllis Webstad
Illustrations: Brock Nicol